W9-AUK-191

Biomedical Engineer

Other titles in the *Cutting Edge Careers* series include:

Big Data Analyst

Cybersecurity Analyst

Video Game Designer

Robotics Engineer

Software Engineer

Virtual Reality Developer

Biomedical Engineer

Bradley Steffens

San Diego, CA

For more information, contact:
ReferencePoint Press, Inc.
PO Box 27779
San Diego, CA 92198
www.ReferencePointPress.com

LIBRARY OF CONGRESS CATALOGING-IN-PUBLICATION DATA

Name: Steffens, Bradley, 1955–
Title: Biomedical engineer/by Bradley Steffens.
Description: San Diego, CA: ReferencePoint Press, Inc., 2018. | Series:
    Cutting edge careers series | Audience: Grade 9 to 12. | Includes
    bibliographical references and index.
Identifiers: LCCN 2016052621 (print) | LCCN 2016053618 (ebook) | ISBN
    9781682821787 (hardback) | ISBN 9781682821794 (eBook)
Subjects: LCSH: Biomedical engineering—Juvenile literature. | Biomedical
    technicians—Vocational guidance—Juvenile literature. | Medical
    technology—Vocational guidance—Juvenile literature.
Classification: LCC R856.2 .S74 2018 (print) | LCC R856.2 (ebook) | DDC
    610.28--dc23
LC record available at https://lccn.loc.gov/2016052621

CONTENTS

BIOMEDICAL ENGINEER AT A GLANCE

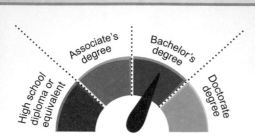

High school diploma or equivalent | Associate's degree | Bachelor's degree | Doctorate degree

Educational Requirements
Bachelor's degree and above

Certification and Licensing

Required for some positions

Working Conditions

Office and Lab

Personal Qualities

☑ Ingenuity

☑ Creativity

☑ Problem-solving skills

Salary $51,500 ⟷ $139,500

22,100

Number of jobs

Growth rate

23%

Future Job Outlook

Source: Bureau of Labor Statistics, *Occupational Outlook Handbook*. www.bls.gov.

Developing Technology to Treat Disease

Technology is revolutionizing the practice of medicine—from advanced research laboratories to everyday medical examination rooms. In research labs, scientists are using high-speed gene sequencing machines to understand how an individual's unique genetic code keeps him or her healthy or allows a disease to take hold and spread throughout the body. In hospitals, surgeons guide tiny robotic arms outfitted with cameras and surgical instruments deep inside patients' bodies to perform delicate operations with greater precision and less trauma than is possible with traditional surgery. In cancer clinics, radiation therapists use linear accelerators to direct high-energy X-rays at cancer cells to shrink or remove them. Across the medical field, doctors and technicians are deploying a dizzying array of medical technologies to provide patients with effective treatments so they can lead longer, healthier lives.

The People Behind the Innovations

Behind every piece of medical equipment is a person who envisioned, designed, or refined the technology. Such men and women are known as biomedical engineers. They apply physics, mathematics, electronics, and chemistry to biological problems to develop new devices, materials, and processes to diagnose and treat diseases. "One could describe [biomedical engineering] as using engineering principles to solve important biomedical or clinical problems," says Joyce Y. Wong, professor of biomedical engineering at Boston University. "To me, the most exciting opportunity is to be presented a problem that a clinician may have, and then being asked to help form a solution."[1]

The field of biomedical engineering is extremely broad. It includes the development of artificial limbs, such as brain-controlled hands and legs, as well as implantable joints, such as hip and knee replacements. It includes the design and manufacture of artificial organs, such as artificial hearts and skin, which are in use today, as well as artificial eyes, lungs, and livers that are currently in development. Some biomedical engineers design diagnostic equipment, such as imaging machines that use sound waves (ultrasound), magnetic resonance (MRI), or radiation (3-D computer tomography), to see inside the body. Other biomedical engineers design drug pumps that can be implanted in a patient's body to deliver medication at the right times and in the right doses.

A Promising Career

Bioengineering is a promising career path for students interested in the sciences. A great deal of money is being invested in biomedicine, because the profits can be astronomical. A successful medical device can generate billions of dollars in sales, in part because people are willing to spend a lot of money on their health, especially for lifesaving treatments. The profitability of the biotechnology market means that bioengineers are highly sought after. In turn, many bioengineers are excited to help create the next big breakthroughs in medical technology.

Another factor in the growth of bioengineering is the sheer size of the market for bioengineered products. According to the Pew Research Center, 18 percent of the US population will be older than sixty-five years by 2025. More older people means more cases of chronic diseases such as Alzheimer's disease and cancer. New and more effective treatments for those and other diseases will be greatly needed, increasing the market for bioengineered products. In addition, older people also require more joint replacements, hearing implants, and other artificial organs and body parts.

The aging population is not the only factor driving the increased need for bioengineers. According to the World Health Organization (WHO), "an escalating global epidemic of overweight and obesity—'globesity'—is taking over many parts of the world. If immediate action is not taken, millions will suffer from an array of serious health disorders."[2] Despite widespread knowledge about nutrition and exercise, obesity has proven nearly impossible to control using traditional methods. However, in May 2016, bioengineers at Massachusetts Institute of Technology (MIT) and Brigham and Women's Hospital announced a novel therapy using nanoparticles (particles measured in billionths of an inch) that reduced the body weight of obese mice by 10 percent over twenty-five days, without side effects. The bioengineers placed two drugs within the nanoparticles that stimulate fat-storing white fat tissue to become fat-burning brown fat tissue. They then placed molecules that bind only to fat tissue on the outside of the nanoparticles. These molecules "guided" the nanoparticles to the white fat tissue, ensuring the drugs reached only the targeted cells. Although the therapy has not yet been tested in humans, it shows how bioengineering may be able to solve a problem that traditional approaches have not. "This is a very exciting and clinically important contribution, grounded in the recognition of the significant and growing need for new therapeutic approaches for the treatment of obesity,"[3] says Marsha Moses, a professor at Harvard Medical School and director of the vascular biology program at Boston Children's Hospital.

Bioengineering is being used to combat not only obesity, but also other diseases such as cancer and diabetes. "My advice to students who are interested in going into biomedical engineering is to not have preconceived notions of what biomedical engineering is," says Wong. "You can even create a new field of biomedical engineering. It really is completely open."[4]

"My advice to students . . . is to not have preconceived notions of what biomedical engineering is. You can even create a new field of biomedical engineering. It really is completely open."[4]

—Joyce Y. Wong, professor of biomedical engineering at Boston University

CHAPTER 1

What Does a Biomedical Engineer Do?

A biomedical engineer seeks to improve human health by integrating engineering principles with biomedical science and clinical practice. Because biomedical engineering combines the knowledge and principles from different disciplines, it is considered an interdisciplinary profession.

The disciplines involved in biomedical engineering are large and varied, making it a very broad field. For example, engineering itself includes many fields, including mechanical engineering, chemical engineering, and electrical engineering. Each of these areas has various specialties. Chemical engineering, for instance, includes fluid dynamics, materials science, molecular engineering, and nanotechnology. Medicine, too, includes various areas of specialization. For example, some researchers might specialize in a particular disease, such as cancer or diabetes, or in a certain bodily system, such as the pulmonary or nervous system.

Specialization

Because of the depth of knowledge needed in each specialty, most bioengineers focus their efforts in one area. Some engineers, for example, specialize in what is called bioinstrumentation, which involves pairing electronics with software programs to design highly sensitive measuring devices that can be used to diagnose and treat disease. At the bioinstrumentation department at the University of California, Berkeley, Michael Yartsev is developing wireless technology to measure the brain activity of bats. "We advance and develop technologies for studying neural activity in freely behaving and flying bats and apply those to our investigation of their neural circuits," says Yartsev. "We aim to uncover basic principles of brain function that are general across mammals."[5]

Some biomedical engineers, known as biomaterials engineers, study how man-made and naturally occurring materials interact with living organisms. "[One] area we have done a lot of work in [is] what I call tissue engineering," says Robert Langer, an institute professor in the Department of Chemical Engineering, Bioengineering, and Mechanical Engineering at MIT. "That's ways of combining cells and materials to someday create new tissues and organs. Like, could you create new skin? A new pancreas? A new liver? New spinal cords? Things like that." Langer also says his department is working on other innovations that may someday reduce or eliminate the need for a patient to take certain kinds of medicine. "We're also combining cells and polymers to create a new pancreas, so if somebody is diabetic, someday, hopefully, we'll be able to have these cells that are encapsulated in a little polymer in [the patient] that could treat them so they wouldn't have to take injections and they'd get better control of their blood glucose levels and hopefully reduce complications."[6]

Some biomedical engineers apply the principles of mechanics to solve medical problems, and they are known as biomechanical engineers. Biomechanical engineers often use Newton's laws of motion or the laws of fluid mechanics to analyze systems in the body. For example, Gilda Barabino, dean of the Grove School of Engineering at The City College of New York, has studied the mechanics of cells and cell behavior, and how the tissues they make up act under the influence of forces in the body. "In that realm," says Barabino, "I've studied sickle cell disease, where we looked at the abnormal mechanics of red blood cells and the mechanics of blood flow."[7]

> "[One] area we have done a lot of work in [is] what I call tissue engineering. That's ways of combining cells and materials to someday create new tissues and organs. Like, could you create new skin? A new pancreas? A new liver? New spinal cords? Things like that."[6]
>
> —Robert Langer, institute professor at MIT

Combining Knowledge

Kay C. Dee, a professor of biomedical engineering at Rose-Hulman Institute of Technology in Indiana, tells the EngineerGirl website how bioengineering combines knowledge from different areas to create new solutions:

My field of expertise is cell and tissue engineering. Cell and tissue engineers combine knowledge from sciences (like biology and chemistry) with principles from traditional engineering fields (like electrical, mechanical, or chemical engineering). The scientific knowledge helps us understand how cells and tissues work; then we use our engineering skills to develop methods to control how the cells and tissues function. For example, understanding how bones heal when they are broken or injured helps me figure out which chemicals in the body "tell" bone cells to make new bone tissue. I can then put similar chemicals on the surface of a biomaterial. A dental or orthopedic implant made out of that biomaterial would "tell" bone cells to make bone at the tissue-implant interface, and the implant would heal quickly and strongly. This is one of the projects I've worked on in my laboratory!

Quoted in National Academy of Engineering, "Interviews: Kay C. Dee," EngineerGirl, January 11, 2008. www.engineergirl.org.

Biomedical engineers who specialize in the area of genetics are known as genetic engineers. These engineers often work at the molecular level, isolating strands of deoxyribonucleic acid (DNA), locating a section of DNA that includes a certain gene, and modifying the gene. For example, a genetic engineer might transplant normal genes into cells that have missing or defective genes in order to treat disorders such as hemophilia, leukemia, immune deficiencies, and Parkinson's disease.

Bioengineers in Hospitals

Some biomedical engineers do not work with the body directly, but instead apply engineering principles to the health care technology that is used in clinical settings, such as hospitals. These engineers are known as clinical engineers. Their job is to acquire, install, and organize medical equipment so it works as well as possible. For example, many types of diagnostic equipment use computers to process patient data. These computers might use different operating and software systems. Clinical engineers often need to integrate the information from the different systems into a single database.

Another kind of biomedical engineer who works in a hospital setting is a medical imaging engineer. Medical imaging has become vital to the practice of medicine because it allows doctors to "see" inside patients to observe tissues and organs that are not functioning properly. Medical imaging engineers develop and refine equipment that uses sound, radiation, or magnetism to produce images of organs and tissues inside the body. "A pioneering piece of technology that we're working on is using ultrasound to look at brain activity. It's called transcranial Doppler ultrasound," explains Tom Chau, vice president of research at Holland Bloorview Kids Rehabilitation Hospital. "We use the Doppler effect to measure the blood flow velocity in some of the major arteries in the brain. What this allows us to do is, for someone who is not able to speak, is not able to move, we can get a sense of when, for example, they're spelling words, or they're imagining shapes rotating in space."[8]

Another kind of engineer—an orthopedic engineer—focuses his or her attention on solving problems of the skeletal muscular system, such as replacing or repairing damaged or diseased bones, cartilage, intervertebral disks, tendons, and ligaments. Some design and test artificial joints to replace ones that have degenerated due to arthritis or injury. Others design and improve prosthetics, such as artificial limbs, including those that can be controlled via electronic signals from the brain. "Brains controlling prosthetic limbs? As an 18-year-old, I wanted to be part of that," says Melanie McWade, vice president of emerging therapies for Nexeon MedSystems in Nashville, Tennessee. "I get to be on the cusp of research and also turn the research into a real commercial product."[9]

> "Brains controlling prosthetic limbs? As an 18-year-old, I wanted to be part of that."[9]
>
> —Melanie McWade, vice president of emerging therapies for Nexeon MedSystems

Rehabilitation engineers seek technological solutions to the problems of people with disabilities. They develop solutions to aid the recovery of physical functions, such as the loss of motor skills, or cognitive functions, such as memory loss.

A Range of Duties

Since biomedical engineering encompasses a wide range of duties and practices, the daily routines of biomedical engineers can vary greatly. Most bioengineers spend at least part of their day keeping up with the latest news in their field, reading research papers or articles in print or electronic form. "I do lots of computer work and reading!" says Katie Hilpisch, a biomedical engineer for medical device manufacturer Medtronic Corporation in Minneapolis, Minnesota. "Data analysis is a huge part of my job. So using software to analyze data and calculate statistics is a big part of my repertoire. And reading. Articles, books—anything that gives you insight into what has already been done or what other people are working on."[10]

If biomedical engineers work in a research lab in a college or university, they might spend time conducting experiments, testing the usefulness of new equipment or biomaterials they have designed. They also might write research papers that detail their findings. Publishing one's work in a scientific journal is one of the most important benchmarks of a successful biomedical engineer who works in an academic environment.

Biomedical engineers who work in the research and development area of a company—such as a medical device manufacturer or a pharmaceutical company—design or refine products made by their employer. A great deal of time must be spent testing new products to make sure they work as designed and continue to work under real-world conditions. An artificial organ or implanted device that wears out ahead of schedule can endanger a patient's life. The same is true for diagnostic equipment or instrumentation. A component that produces a false reading or test result can pose a danger to a patient's health.

Biomedical engineers must keep extensive records of their work. The Food and Drug Administration (FDA), which must ap-

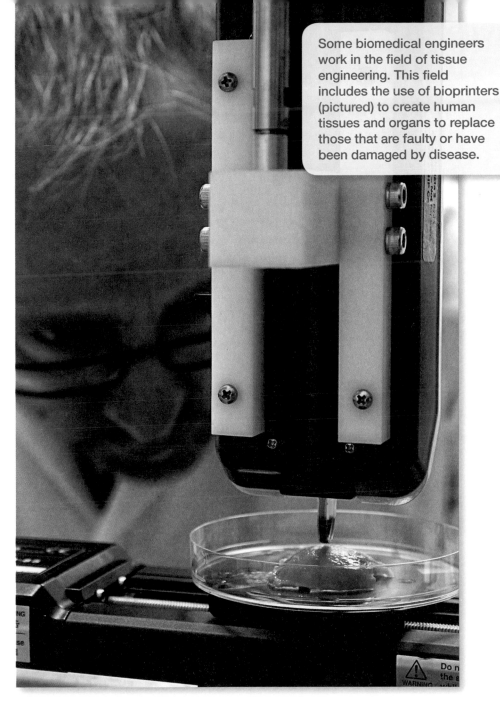

Some biomedical engineers work in the field of tissue engineering. This field includes the use of bioprinters (pictured) to create human tissues and organs to replace those that are faulty or have been damaged by disease.

prove every drug and medical device before it is offered for sale, conducts extensive reviews of new and updated medical products to ensure they are safe and effective. The regulators review the tests on patients, known as clinical trials, as well as the procedures the biomedical engineers followed throughout the product's development. Should there be a problem with a product after its release, the FDA will investigate what went wrong. Bioengineers are often at the forefront of such investigations. Similarly, if dissatisfied or injured patients bring a lawsuit against a medical manufacturer for a faulty product, the attorneys will focus on developing and testing the product, trying to establish whether corners were cut or warning signs ignored. Biomedical engineers must be able to document each step they took to demonstrate that they used sound engineering practices and were not reckless or negligent in their work.

How Do You Become a Biomedical Engineer?

Because biomedical engineering encompasses many fields, those who pursue this career come from a range of educational backgrounds. "There are many paths that lead to a career in biomedical engineering," says Tom Chau. He continues:

> We need the brains and the expertise of many different people, many different disciplines. So as long as you're really good at what you do, you don't have to worry about "Oh, I didn't choose this field or that field." It doesn't matter. I've had students from kinesiology, life sciences, biology, civil engineering, chemical engineering, aerospace engineering— anything you can think of. We've had students come to us, and each of them have brought a unique skill set that has really added value to our work.[11]

High School Preparation

The one subject area that all biomedical engineers—and engineers in general— must master is mathematics. To solve a complex real-world problem, engineers often break the problem down into smaller components that can be analyzed mathematically. The strength of materials, the movement of fluids, the transfer of heat—these and many other physical processes can all be described with mathematical equations. Students interested in any form of engineering must study algebra, geometry, trigonometry,

> "There are many paths that lead to a career in biomedical engineering. We need the brains and the expertise of many different people, many different disciplines."[11]
>
> —Tom Chau, vice president of research at Holland Bloorview Kids Rehabilitation Hospital

Biomedical Engineering Undergraduate Coursework

Johns Hopkins University is often ranked first or second in the nation for its biomedical engineering program. Its undergraduate program includes a set of "core knowledge" that the faculty believes future biomedical engineers should possess. The coursework includes:

- **Basic Sciences,** including General Physics, Introductory Chemistry, and Organic Chemistry
- **Mathematics,** including Calculus I, II, III, Linear Algebra, Differential Equations, and Statistics
- **Humanities and Social Sciences,** such as history, philosophy, psychology, anthropology, all arranged in a coherent program that is relevant to the student's goals
- **Biomedical Core Knowledge**:
  - Biomedical Modeling and Design
  - Biomedical Engineering in the Real World
  - Molecules and Cells
  - Biomedical Systems and Controls—analysis of biological control systems
  - Biomedical Models and Simulations—analysis of systems described by linear and nonlinear ordinary differential equations

calculus, and statistics. Most, if not all of these subjects, can be taken at the high school level. At the college level, engineering students often study mathematical engineering, a branch of applied mathematics focused on methods and techniques typically used in engineering and industry.

Science is the other main subject area useful to students who want to become biomedical engineers. The life sciences, such as biology and physiology, provide a background in some of the medical processes that a biomedical engineer might work with later. Chemistry and physics also are valuable for a biomedical engineering student. Since computers are used in practically ev-

- Statistical Mechanics and Thermodynamics
- Systems Bioengineering I: Cells and Cardiovascular Systems
- Systems Bioengineering II: Neural Systems
- Systems Bioengineering III: Genes to Organs

- **Focus Areas:**
  - Systems Biology
  - Sensors, Micro/Nano Systems, and Instrumentation
  - Cell/Tissue Engineering and Biomaterials
  - Computational Bioengineering
  - Imaging

- **Design:**
  - Senior Design in Materials Science & Engineering
  - Advanced Electronics Laboratory
  - Control Systems Design
  - Microfabrication Lab

- **Computer Programming,** featuring programming languages such as MATLAB, Python, and Java

- **General Electives** that are appropriate to the student's interests, such as premedical courses, double majors, minors, music, language, research, or business

Johns Hopkins Biomedical Engineering, "Bachelors of Science Degree Requirements." www.bme.jhu.edu.

ery area of biomedical engineering, being familiar with computer science, computational methods, and programming can be helpful to the aspiring biomedical engineer. Even if engineers do not do the programming or computational analysis themselves, understanding computing will help them communicate with the software engineers, systems engineers, or database administrators who will likely be part of the team on which they will work.

A student who hopes to design medical devices, prosthetics, or artificial organs will also benefit from taking basic design courses such as drafting, mechanical drawing, and computer graphics.

College Preparation

Biomedical engineers need to have at least a bachelor's degree in engineering or biomedical engineering to get an entry-level job in the field. Students who major in life sciences or another nonengineering field for their undergraduate degree will need to study engineering at the graduate level if they want to become biomedical engineers. Students must make sure the engineering program they pursue is accredited by the Accreditation Board for Engineering and Technology (ABET), the leading engineering accreditation organization in the United States.

Biomedical engineering is a relatively new field, and thus many undergraduate programs in biomedical engineering are new. As a result many practicing biomedical engineers first studied another field. "When I got started, biomedical engineering as a field and as a discipline wasn't as well developed, so I did my graduate work in chemical engineering," says Gilda Barabino. "I applied chemical engineering principles to problems in medicine, and in particular sickle cell disease."[12]

Biomedical engineering programs are multidisciplinary. They include engineering courses, such as fluid mechanics, solid mechanics, and engineering design. They also include life sciences courses, such as biology, anatomy, and physiology. They often include basic science courses such as chemistry and physics. Many programs include computing courses, such as programming and circuit design. A background in computing will help biomedical engineers employ computational thinking to solve some of the challenges they face and to integrate electronics into their designs where necessary.

Volunteer Opportunities and Internships

An important part of any science major is laboratory work, and biomedical engineering is no exception. Biomedical engineers spend many hours in labs learning the proper ways to design, conduct, and analyze experiments. Many biomedical engineering students gain laboratory experience by working in a professional lab as a volunteer or intern. The Biomedical Engineering

Society (BMES), a society of professionals devoted to developing and using engineering and technology to advance human health, provides volunteer opportunities and internships for biomedical students to gain work experience, expand their knowledge, and build their skills.

Private companies, colleges, universities, and government-run labs offer internships as well. For example, the National Institute of Biomedical Imaging and Bioengineering, part of the National Institutes of Health (NIH), sponsors a Biomedical Engineering Summer Internship for undergraduate biomedical engineering students who have completed their junior year of college. The ten-week program allows senior bioengineering students to participate in biomedical research projects under the mentorship of scientists in NIH laboratories in Bethesda, Maryland.

"When I got started, biomedical engineering as a field and as a discipline wasn't as well developed, so I did my graduate work in chemical engineering. I applied chemical engineering principles to problems in medicine, and in particular sickle cell disease."[12]

—Gilda Barabino, dean of the Grove School of Engineering at The City College of New York

A Master's or a PhD Program

A bachelor's degree in biomedical engineering is often enough for a graduate to be hired for an entry-level position with a medical device manufacturer or pharmaceutical company. However, a position in a research lab, especially at a college or university, will require a master's degree or a PhD. This has less to do with the engineering part of the job than with the science. A biomedical engineer working with genes, stem cells, proteins, biomaterials, or other complex biological systems must have a deep understanding of the science behind the technology. This kind of in-depth education is available mainly at the graduate and postgraduate level.

A master's degree program is usually a two-year course of study focused on a specific field of study or area of professional practice. Students pursuing a master's degree in biomedical engineering are taught the traditional engineering disciplines, such as chemical engineering and mechanical engineering. They also

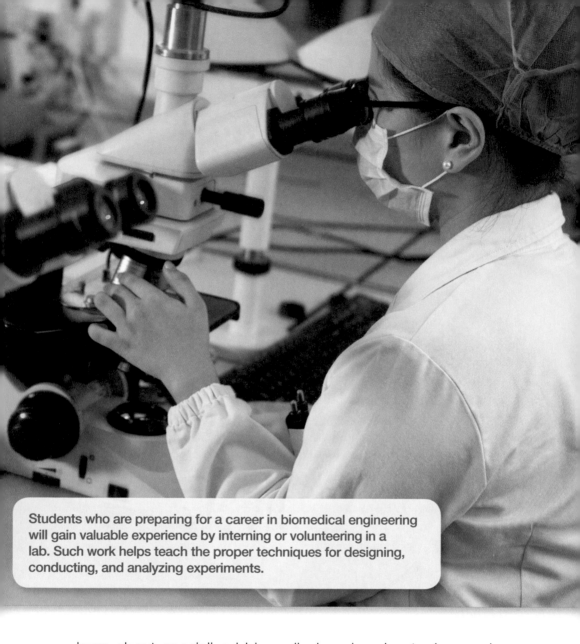

Students who are preparing for a career in biomedical engineering will gain valuable experience by interning or volunteering in a lab. Such work helps teach the proper techniques for designing, conducting, and analyzing experiments.

learn about specialized biomedical engineering topics, such as genetic engineering, bioinstrumentation, tissue engineering, or clinical engineering. Master's degree students usually complete a thesis, a paper that presents the author's research and findings. A biomedical engineering thesis is often based on a research topic that requires the application of quantitative or applied engineering principles to biomedical engineering.

A master's degree normally precedes, and is a requirement for enrolling in, a doctor of philosophy, or PhD, program. A PhD program typically lasts four to five years. It involves high-level coursework as well as a great deal of laboratory research under the guidance of a professor known as a faculty adviser. For example, biomedical doctoral candidates at Columbia University are expected to complete thirty credits beyond the master's degree. However, up to twenty-one of the credits can be in research conducted under the supervision of the faculty adviser. At the end of the PhD program, the candidate must pass an oral examination, a written examination, and submit and defend a dissertation—a very in-depth paper based on the candidate's individual research.

Certification and Licensing

Some biomedical engineers are self-employed and offer their services directly to clients. To do so, most states require that they be licensed. Licensing protects the public by restricting the practice of engineering to individuals who have met specific qualifications in education, work experience, and exams. Many state licensing boards require engineers to renew their licenses throughout their careers to demonstrate their ongoing professional competency.

Most states require engineers to pass exams administered by the National Council of Examiners for Engineering and Surveying (NCEES), a nonprofit organization dedicated to advancing professional licensure for engineers and surveyors. NCEES offers two basic exams: Fundamentals of Engineering (FE) exam for recent graduates and Principles and Practice of Engineering (PE) exam for people with four years of work experience. NCEES offers exams for many kinds of engineers—mechanical engineers, civil engineers, aeronautical engineers—but it does not yet offer a PE exam for biomedical engineers. A biomedical engineer seeking licensure through NCEES must pass an exam in another specialty, such as agricultural and biological engineering, chemical engineering, mechanical systems and materials engineering, or thermal and fluids systems engineering. Those who pass the PE exam are licensed as professional engineers.

Biomedical engineers who do not offer their services to the public but instead work for private companies, institutions of higher learning, or government laboratories normally are not required to be licensed. However, twelve states require that biomedical engineers who have contact with medical patients—during clinical trials, for example—be licensed: California, Florida, Georgia, Hawaii, Louisiana, Montana, Nevada, New York, North Dakota, Rhode Island, Tennessee, and West Virginia. Health care licensing is available through the various state boards of occupational licensure or departments of health. Requirements vary from state to state, but they can include proof of college degree, a certain amount of work experience, and passing a written exam.

What Skills and Personal Qualities Are Important to a Biomedical Engineer?

Since bioengineering is a broad, interdisciplinary field, it attracts people with many different skills and personal qualities. Some may have excellent math or computing skills, while others may excel in biology or chemistry. Those who design new devices may be highly creative, while those who test those devices may have outstanding analytical skills. Different jobs require different skills and qualities, and different skills and qualities may lead to very different careers.

A Desire to Help Others

One personal quality shared by a large number of biomedical engineers is a desire to help other people. "I learned that one of the things I did like to do was to help people," says Gilda Barabino. "In particular, I was interested in applications that would improve human health, so what better field than biomedical engineering?"[13]

Fernando Cordova, a biomedical engineer with Brainlab, Inc., provides clinical and technical support to surgeons. He, too, takes satisfaction in the fact that he is helping people in his work. "I have friends who are marketers that went into business," he says. "They talk about cool things they did at work. My cool thing that I did at work was I helped the surgeon save someone's life. I don't think there's anything more rewarding than that."[14]

Having an impact on human lives also drew Ravi Bellamkonda, chair of the biomedical engineering department at Georgia Tech and Emory University and president of the American Institute for Medical and Biological Engineering, into biomedical engineering. "Inherently there is meaning in what I do," says Bellamkonda. "Would I like a better smartphone? Yes. Would I like Wi-Fi everywhere in the world? Yes. But, if something that I do helps a child who has a cancer that couldn't be treated otherwise, I would take that any day. If I can make a difference in such an arena, you can see that it could be very, very rewarding."[15]

Robert Langer came to the same conclusion during the first job he held after receiving his PhD, known as a postdoctoral position:

> When I graduated from MIT, I began to work at Boston Children's Hospital. I was probably the only engineer in the entire hospital, and I got to see all kinds of medical problems: What ways could you stop blood vessels? Could we create new materials? Could we remove things that were bad from the body? Could we deliver drugs in better ways? . . . I started to realize that there are all of these problems that chemical engineers really had not dealt with, and since I had learned something about chemical engineering, I thought, well, maybe I can help solve some of those.[16]

Creative Problem Solving

In addition to sharing a desire to help people with medical conditions, most biomedical engineers also have excellent problem-solving skills. They typically are able to understand a problem at a

One possible outcome of combining biology and engineering is a greater likelihood of new treatments and cures for brain disease. People who develop tumors, hemorrhages, and other conditions shown in these brain scans could benefit from the work of biomedical engineers (opposite page).

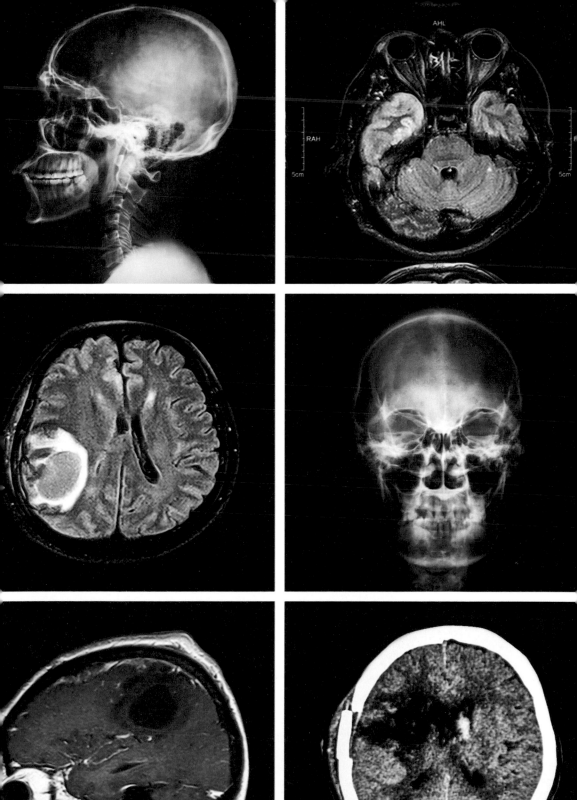

physical or chemical level and then see how the problem relates to a larger biological system. "One of the ways engineers address complex problems is to first break them down into parts, and then put those parts back together and come up with the solutions that are relevant," says Barabino.[17]

Biomedical engineers also need to be able to think creatively. That often means being willing to challenge accepted ideas about how things function. It also means combining existing information in new ways to create innovative equipment, devices, and therapies. "I find one of the best ways to come up with a new approach is to take the ideas in one area and apply them

"Don't Be Intimidated"

In a video for the American Institute for Medical and Biological Engineering, Ravi Bellamkonda, the president of the organization, advises students contemplating biomedical engineering to not be intimidated by science:

If you look at science, my message is: Please don't be intimidated by it. Science is just curiosity, and following your curiosity, using some methodological approaches. If you are a curious individual and wonder why something is the way it is—why is the sky blue? or why this a certain way?—science is your friend, because that's the way you find out. Yes, we use math. Yes, we use biology. We use all these things, but those are all for our convenience to try to find out. It is not an end. . . . Don't think that math is science, or biology is science. That is not science. Science is just following your curiosity in some organized way. And there are tools that help you follow it—biology, math, physics, and all these things, but at the end of the day you're trying to find out how something is. If you allow yourself to be curious, you are a scientist in your own way, whether you are trained to be one or not.

Quoted in American Institute for Medical and Biological Engineering, "Ravi Bellamkonda Interview," Meet Inspiring Bioengineers. http://navigate.aimbe.org.

in a different area," says Barabino. "We are an interdisciplinary field by nature, but the most significant advances that we're seeing are coming at the intersection of different disciplines within our discipline. So maybe you have a biological concept that you then apply an engineering concept to. That's where you're making the real discovery."[18]

Bellamkonda offers an example of how biology and engineering can be creatively brought together to fight brain cancer. This disease is very challenging to treat because brain tumors, especially aggressive ones, tend not to stay put in the brain. Rather, they move around, and particularly tend to move along nearby nerves or blood vessels. In thinking about this problem, Bellamkonda says, "We had this idea—perhaps crazy—of thinking: 'Hey, could it be that tumors like to grow along these fiber-like structural features, that there isn't some biology that's attracting them to grow somewhere?' They just latch onto these things like you would drive on a highway. There's a road; you want to go on it." Bellamkonda's team thought if that was true, perhaps they could design their own "highway" to which the tumors could attach— something they could control. "So we . . . designed structures made out of polymers—an artificial construct—and were able to direct the cancer to come out of the brain on its own," explains Bellamkonda. He continues:

> This is a case where an engineer—this is one of those things that only an engineer would be crazy enough to try—thinks about cancer in a very different way. We're not looking for a new drug. In fact, this is a case where the cancer comes to your drug, because you can make the tumor come out and capture it in [a] drug depot or something, instead of the drug going in and killing normal cells in your brain.[19]

Math and Science

While compassion, problem solving, and creativity are vital to being a biomedical engineer, the career also demands sound engineering skills, which in turn are based largely on physics and math. Engineers need to be skilled in geometry and trigonometry to understand such things as mechanics and fluid dynamics. They need to understand calculus so they can mathematically model optimal solutions. They may need a good grasp of statistics to analyze complex biological systems. "The advice I would give to anyone who is contemplating a career in biomedical engineering is that it is engineering," says Bellamkonda. "It sounds great: You want to invent new things. But there are many other fields that let you do that without math and physics. If you don't like math and physics—you don't have to be the best at it, but you need to be decent at it—if you don't like that, then this is a tough field," Bellamkonda explains. "It is, after all, engineering. It is not just biology."[20]

> "To be a good engineer, you have to be able to explain things to other people. The best engineering ideas in the world won't do anyone any good if you can't get other people to understand them and use them!"[22]
>
> —Kay C. Dee, professor of biomedical engineering at Rose-Hulman Institute of Technology in Indiana

Computing skills are important for biomedical engineers in many areas. They are essential for creating instruments, diagnostic equipment, and medical devices that include small data-processing components. They also are vital for conducting computer modeling to analyze biological systems, such as interactions between various proteins. In addition, computing can be used to create simulations that show how to design or modify devices for optimum performance. A clinical engineer needs programming and operating skills to upgrade devices and equipment in a hospital setting.

Communicating the Solutions

Biomedical engineers often work in teams, and this requires good communication skills. "I work with all levels," explains Lori Laird, a biomedical engineer for Guidant Corporation, a medical device firm in Santa Clara, California. "I have two technicians that report to me. I work with them almost on a daily basis, giving them jobs to do [and] keeping them updated on things that are going on. I work with managers, I work with directors. Every once in a while,

I'll be able to speak to a doctor to have his input on things. Having good communication skills allows you to work with such a broad range of people."[21]

Biomedical engineers also need good writing skills to present their ideas to nonengineers in reports, to write grant proposals to secure funding, and to write papers for scientific journals. "People always say that they became engineers because they like math and science—well, I like science, but I also like writing, and reading, and music, and art. I think the things I've learned about communicating with people (writing, talking, listening, drawing, demonstrating) make me a more effective engineer and a more effective teacher," says Kay C. Dee, a professor of biomedical engineering at Rose-Hulman Institute of Technology in Indiana. "To be a good engineer, you have to be able to explain things to other people. The best engineering ideas in the world won't do anyone any good if you can't get other people to understand them and use them!"[22]

What Is It Like to Work as a Biomedical Engineer?

Because biomedical engineering is a broad field, biomedical engineers work in several different industries and earn a range of salaries. According to the Bureau of Labor Statistics (BLS), twenty-two thousand biomedical engineers were employed in 2014. Most of these were concentrated in five industries: medical equipment and supplies manufacturing; research and development; pharmaceutical manufacturing; measuring, electromedical, and instruments manufacturing; and hospitals.

Working in the Medical Equipment Sector

The largest percentage of biomedical engineers—23 percent—works for medical equipment and supplies manufacturers, yet even this is a diverse field. Some biomedical engineers work for companies that produce or are developing artificial organs, such as hearts, lungs, and livers. Others work for companies that make artificial joints, such as hips, or artificial disks to replace those between vertebrae in the spine. Some work on the development of artificial limbs, such as legs, arms, and hands. Biomedical engineers are also involved in developing and refining implantable devices, such as stents that keep blood vessels open.

Medical equipment manufacturers also make robotic equipment that surgeons use to operate on patients with greater precision and less trauma to the body than traditional surgery allows. In the most common type of robot-assisted surgery, known as remote surgery, the surgeon sits at a computer console near the operating table. The console includes a telemanipulator, which relays the movements of the surgeon's hands to tiny robotic arms located near the operating table. One arm is equipped with a camera and others have surgical instruments attached to them. Watching a high-definition, 3-D view from the robotic camera, the surgeon guides the robotic arms through a small incision to the site of the surgery and performs the procedure. Biomedical engineers not only developed the first of these machines, but are also constantly at work to improve them.

Working in Research and Development

According to the BLS about 16 percent of biomedical engineers work in research and development laboratories. This is another broad category. Some work with the human genome in a field known as genomics; some study the interactions of proteins in a field known as proteomics. Those in a field known as metabolomics study metabolites—molecules created within a cell as a result of certain cellular processes—to better understand how cells function. Some work with stem cells, which have the capacity to grow into any kind of organ or tissue, and still others work in nanomedicine, using structures so small they can easily penetrate the walls of cells.

Bioengineering in the Pharmaceutical Industry

About 12 percent of biomedical engineers work in the pharmaceutical, or drug, industry. Some bioengineers, like the team at MIT and Brigham and Women's Hospital that used nanoparticles to deliver drugs to fat tissue, are exploring ways to use nanotechnology to deliver drugs like chemotherapy (which is used to treat cancer) into a person's system in ways that maximize harm to the diseased tissue but minimize harm to the rest of the body. "We use nanotechnology to deliver a drug and put the entire chemotherapy hopefully only to the tumor so the body is spared the toxic side-effects of chemotherapy," says Robert Langer. "The drug just goes right to the tumor."[23]

Nanotechnology is not the only frontier in drug delivery. Biomedical engineers are also combining microelectronics with drug

A Day in the Life of a Biomedical Engineer

Lori Laird is a biomedical engineer for Guidant Corporation, a medical device firm located in Santa Clara, California. She discussed her typical day on the TryEngineering website:

> What's my day like? Let's see. Yesterday was a good day. I started out checking out email and voice mail and writing myself my "to do" list for today; these are the things I'm going to accomplish. I went to a meeting in the morning. After that, I went to a class where they teach about the safety of blood-borne pathogens. In medical devices, there are a lot of safety and medical issues. We handle devices as they come back from the field to check them out for defects and things like that. And I took a class on how to handle the devices and not get contaminated by the blood. After that, I checked out one of the tools. We're having a problem with one of our tools on the manufacturing line. So I sat down [and] . . . did a little bit of designing. Not a lot of design work. . . . We've done most of the designing already. So a lot of our stuff is just the manufacturing part of it.

Quoted in TryEngineering, "Lori Laird: Biomedical Engineer." www.tryengineering.org.

delivery. "We've created these microchips that you can put different drugs in, and you can actually put these in the body and even deliver them [the drugs] by remote control," says Langer. "Someday we're going to have little sensors in these chips so the chips themselves will be able to sense things in the human body and deliver them, depending on what those signals are."[24] Biomedical engineers also work on more standard drug delivery systems, such as inhalers, external drug pumps that patients can activate as needed, and implantable drug pumps that automatically release the correct dose of medication at the correct time.

Working with Electronics

About 8 percent of biomedical engineers work in measuring, electromedical, and instruments manufacturing, according to the BLS. This includes work on implantable electrical devices such as pacemakers, which regulate the heartbeat. It also includes work on equipment used outside the body to help doctors diagnose and treat diseases. For example, technicians known as sonographers use equipment called ultrasound machines to create images of organs and tissues beneath the skin. The technicians place an instrument called an ultrasound transducer onto the skin of a patient and direct high-frequency sound waves (inaudible to human beings) into the body. The various tissues inside the body reflect some of the sound waves back to the probe, which relays the "echo" information to the ultrasound machine. The machine uses sophisticated software to plot these echoes on a screen, creating a two-dimensional image of what is beneath the skin. By "seeing" inside the body, doctors can more accurately diagnose certain problems. Bioengineers are continually seeking to improve the sensitivity and accuracy of such equipment.

Another 8 percent of biomedical engineers work in hospitals as clinical engineers. These engineers are familiar with all kinds of equipment used in clinical settings. They install, maintain, and optimize the equipment for ease of use and maximum patient benefit. Sometimes they train doctors, technicians, and other clinical personnel in how to use the equipment.

Work Environment

Biomedical engineers work indoors in a range of settings—offices, laboratories, production facilities, and clinical settings. Most spend the majority of their time in their offices, reading about the latest research in their specialty, e-mailing research collaborators or other members of their research or product team, analyzing problems they are trying to solve, and designing solutions by hand or on a computer. They may spend time in a laboratory performing experiments that help them further understand the problem they are trying to solve, or testing their solutions to see how they work. "I would say a good 75 percent of my time is spent at my desk, working on the computer," says Katie Hilpisch. "The other 25 percent is spent in research labs or hospitals doing, well, research!"[25]

If the bioengineer works at a manufacturer, he or she might spend time in the factory where the products are made to better understand problems the production team is having with making a piece of equipment the engineer has designed. Sometimes biomedical engineers meet with doctors and patients to better understand the problems they are trying to solve. "Doctors will come in and they'll tell you, 'We're having difficulty with this type of surgery and we'd like to develop a better way to do this surgery,'" says Lori Laird. "So immediately we hit the drawing board and say, okay, how can we develop a product to do this?"[26]

Biomedical engineers usually work full time on a normal schedule. However, they sometimes must work evenings and weekends to meet deadlines or to monitor experiments or tests that cannot be stopped once they are under way. For example, a bioengineer using robotic equipment to sort cells according to the proteins on the outside of the cells—a process known as cell cytometry—might need to monitor the equipment until the sorting is complete to make sure everything is working properly.

> "I would say a good 75 percent of my time is spent at my desk, working on the computer. The other 25 percent is spent in research labs or hospitals doing, well, research!"[25]
>
> —Katie Hilpisch, biomedical engineer for Medtronic Corporation

A Well-Paying Profession

Given the extensive schooling and high-level skills that are involved in this field, biomedical engineers earn incomes far above the national average of all occupations. According to the BLS, the median annual wage for biomedical engineers was $86,220 in May 2015. That is 2.38 times as much as the median annual wage for all occupations. The lowest 10 percent of biomedical engineers earned less than $51,500 per year, while the highest 10 percent earned more than $139,500.

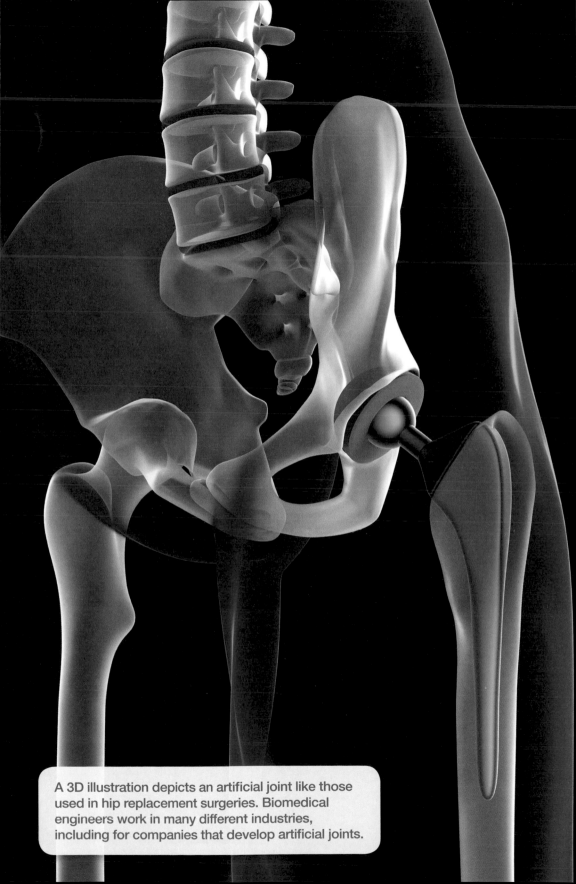

A 3D illustration depicts an artificial joint like those used in hip replacement surgeries. Biomedical engineers work in many different industries, including for companies that develop artificial joints.

The median incomes of biomedical engineers vary, depending on which industry they are in. According to the BLS, in May 2015, those working in the medical equipment and supplies manufacturing sector earned a median annual wage 11 percent greater than those in the pharmaceutical industry—$91,030 compared to $81,750. It is not just the industry, but also the nature of the work that dictates the salary. Those exploring the frontiers of biomedical technology are paid much more than those who work with technology that already exists. For example, biomedical engineers working in research and development earned a median annual wage 33 percent greater than clinical engineers working in hospitals—$97,100 compared to $72,950.

CHAPTER 5

Advancement and Other Job Opportunities

Employed across several different industries, bioengineers follow a variety of career paths. Those employed in colleges and universities will follow an academic career path, while those in private industry, such as medical device manufacturing or the pharmaceutical industry, follow the business organizational path. Those employed in government laboratories might follow more of a scientific career path.

Engineers in Academia

Biomedical engineers who work in a college or university laboratory are usually required to have a PhD. The academic career path is clearly defined, with the publication of research papers being an essential benchmark for promotion. Their careers begin as postdoctoral researchers, or postdocs, in a research laboratory. A postdoc conducts research under the direction of more senior biomedical engineers, performing tests, reading and gathering data, and overseeing the work of technical support staff and students. A postdoc often will collaborate with other members of the laboratory to publish papers about their findings in peer-reviewed journals. The postdoc will be first author on any paper resulting from his or her postdoctoral research.

After publishing research papers, a postdoc often may be hired as an assistant professor. Assistant professors publish scholarly papers, present their research findings at professional conferences, and develop research collaborations. Academic biomedical engineers usually spend time applying for grants to fund their research. Often they are required to fund part or all of their salaries through grants from external sources.

Further publications can lead to a promotion to associate professor. The next step—normally after several years of experience and many publications—is to become a full professor. A full professor normally directs a number of associate professors working in a specific area of research. A full professor can eventually become a department chair, who is responsible for the overall functioning and output of the department.

Biomedical engineers who work in an academic setting have a responsibility to serve the school and its students. This may involve teaching, mentoring, or advising students. It also may involve serving on academic committees, research ethics boards, or the editorial boards of scholarly journals. "When I completed my studies in chemical engineering, I wasn't quite sure if I wanted an academic career path or a career path in industry," says Gilda Barabino. "Where my heart really lay was in working with students in an academic environment and pursuing research directions I was most interested in."[27]

> "I wasn't quite sure if I wanted an academic career path or a career path in industry. Where my heart really lay was in working with students in an academic environment and pursuing research directions I was most interested in."[27]
>
> —Gilda Barabino, dean of the Grove School of Engineering at The City College of New York

Biomedical engineers who work in a research laboratory funded by the government often are referred to as scientists, rather than engineers. They have a career path similar to those in academia, but with different job titles: scientist instead of assistant professor, senior scientist instead of associate professor, principal investigator instead of professor, and group leader instead of department chair. Some laboratories are led by a chief scientist. The career path is clearly defined, with publications and patents serving as the benchmarks for promotion. Biomedical engineers who work in such laboratories do not have responsibilities toward students, except through internship programs.

Opportunities in the Private Sector

Biomedical engineers employed in the many industries across the private sector have a variety of job titles and career paths. They might be a research and development engineer, a manufacturing engineer, or a design quality engineer—all of which are involved with the development of new products and technologies. The career path might be as simple as engineer to senior engineer and then to principal engineer. Such advancement is usually based on years of experience and the number of successful projects the biomedical engineer has completed. The engineer's number of publications and patents also might affect his or her promotion from one level to the next.

Depending on which industry a biomedical engineering graduate enters, the entry-level position might vary. A medical device or equipment manufacturer might hire a recent graduate as a technical support specialist, field agent, or application consultant. Biomedical engineers in these positions are responsible for installing and maintaining medical equipment in health care settings, training medical staff to use the equipment, and even helping physicians operate the equipment during complicated procedures.

A biomedical engineer also might join a company as a regulatory affairs specialist, specializing in obtaining FDA approval for new and modified medical devices and drugs. Regulatory affairs specialists often meet with government officials to discuss testing requirements for new products, respond to FDA requests for information, and track the progress of the product review. Once a drug or device is approved, the regulatory affairs specialist will report on product usage, including any problems that might have arisen. They will also be involved with inspections of the finished product and the manufacturing process.

Blending Engineering with Business

Some biomedical engineers also study business in college. They might even pursue a master's in business administration (MBA).

A Bioengineer in the Operating Room

Fernando Cordova is a senior application consultant for Brainlab, Inc., which makes image-guided therapy tools for use in neurosurgery. He discussed his entry-level position in a video for the American Institute for Medical and Biological Engineering (AIMBE):

> I help neurosurgeons do their job. I make sure they have the right instruments that they need. I make sure they have the right information that they need. I make sure that if they have a great idea for novel research on neurosurgery, spine surgery, ENT surgery . . . , I am able to take that idea and adapt it for what they want to do. So I get to do very simple things in the OR [operating room], and then I get to do real high-level thinking, where I do research and papers and studies and presentations. I cover a big variety of things. . . . They can talk to me about anatomy, molecular imaging, basic mechanics, networks in the hospital, and how a certain software will communicate with another certain software. We can talk about a range of ideas, and I know exactly what we're talking about throughout the way. They know that if they come to me with a problem, I'll get it done, because I have the resources. It's funny, but it all ties back to biomedical engineering.

Quoted in American Institute for Medical and Biological Engineering, "Fernando Cordova Interview," Meet Inspiring Bioengineers. http://navigate.aimbe.org.

Such engineers might move into corporate management positions, overseeing the development of a product line or taking part in strategic product planning. They also might pursue more business-oriented engineering positions, such as business development associate. These engineers obtain, study, and evaluate products developed outside the company for possible licensing or purchase. The biomedical engineering background is vital because the business development associate also must evaluate the company's ability to efficiently develop, produce, and launch the product. A business background is essential, because he or she must assess the cost of bringing such products to market as well as the value of potential sales to determine if the venture will be profitable.

Procurement engineer is another position that requires both an engineering and a business background. Procurement engineers purchase the raw materials or manufactured components a company needs to manufacture its products. Procurement engineers must have a technical understanding of their own company's designs and their materials requirements. They also need the business savvy to evaluate and negotiate purchase agreements with existing suppliers and new bidders. Procurement engineers often travel to meet with suppliers and visit their production plants around the world.

Other Career Directions

Biomedical engineers who have passed the NCEES exam and are licensed as professional engineers can open their own businesses and work for themselves. They might serve as a consultant to individual companies that are shorthanded, or they might work for a consulting firm that offers their services as part of a package to develop or update a product. The self-employed engineer must be skilled at marketing his or her services and finding new clients to stay busy. However, if a self-employed engineer works for a consulting firm, the firm will find the clients and pay the engineer a salary as long as the projects last. Once a project is complete, the consulting firm will typically move the engineer to a new project.

Biomedical engineers who have good communication skills and enjoy working with young people can become teachers. Depending on the degree they hold and state requirements for teaching, they can teach at technical schools, two-year colleges, or at the four-year college level. Biomedical engineers might have several reasons for wanting to teach. They might prefer the security of the education profession to the ups and downs of the business world. During a recession, companies often cut research and development budgets and staff. However, many individuals turn to teaching because they wish to give back to the community, helping to guide and inspire the next generation of biomedical engineers. "My favorite thing about my job is interacting with my students," says Kay C. Dee. "They are interesting, bright, hard-working, and it's a privilege and an honor to get to teach them things about the world."[28]

What Does the Future Hold for Biomedical Engineers?

People who pursue a career in biomedical engineering are nearly guaranteed a well-paying, stable, and rewarding career. According to the BLS, employment of biomedical engineers is projected to grow 23 percent from 2014 to 2024. That rate not only is three times faster than the average for all occupations (7 percent), but it is also nearly six times faster than the average of all other engineering positions (4 percent). The BLS forecasts that the number of biomedical engineering jobs will grow from 22,100 to 27,200 between 2014 and 2024, adding a total of 5,100 new positions. In 2015 CNN Money ranked biomedical engineering at number thirty-seven on its annual list of the "100 Best Jobs in America"—the highest ranking achieved by any engineering profession.

The health care industry, which includes biomedical engineering, is resilient as well. Between 2004 and 2014—a period that includes the "great recession" of 2008, in which many people lost their jobs—employment in health care occupations grew by more than 20 percent, while employment in all other occupations grew by only 3 percent during the same time period.

The growth trend is continuing. According to the Bureau of Economic Analysis, the US economy grew at a meager rate of 0.8 percent in the first quarter of 2016, while the health care sector grew at a rate nearly five times faster than the economy overall—3.8 percent. The Office of the Actuary of the Centers for Medicare & Medicaid Services, a bureau within the Department of Health and Human Services, forecasts that expenditures on health care services will grow at an average rate of 5.8 percent per year between 2015 and 2025, about 1.3 percent higher than projected annual growth in the US gross domestic product. By 2025, health care spending will comprise 20.1 percent of the entire US economy, up from 17.5 percent in 2014. A significant portion of this spending will be on bioengineered products and therapies.

Growth Factors

There are many reasons why the future of biomedical engineering is bright. One is demographics: The number of people who need biomedical products is growing faster than the population at large. Older people need more prosthetics, medical devices, and advanced therapies than younger people do; and the number of older Americans is growing at an astronomical rate. According to the Pew Research Center, ten thousand Americans turn sixty-five years old each day. The growth in older Americans is due to the aging of the World War II baby-boom generation—people born between 1945 and 1965. Because of this population "bubble," the rate of people turning sixty-five will continue for the next fourteen years.

Not only is the American population aging, but older people today are also more determined to stay active than earlier generations were. This fact is helping to drive the growth in the health care industry in general and the medical device industry in particular. Older people are demanding procedures such as hip and knee replacements so they can maintain their active lifestyles during their retirement years. They also are demanding artificial organs, such as cochlear implants to combat hearing loss.

The Demand for Innovative Treatment

Diseases such as cancer, Alzheimer's disease, and heart disease also are prevalent among older people; and demands for better treatments are on the rise. Advanced therapies such as gene and stem cell therapy are not only reported on in traditional me-

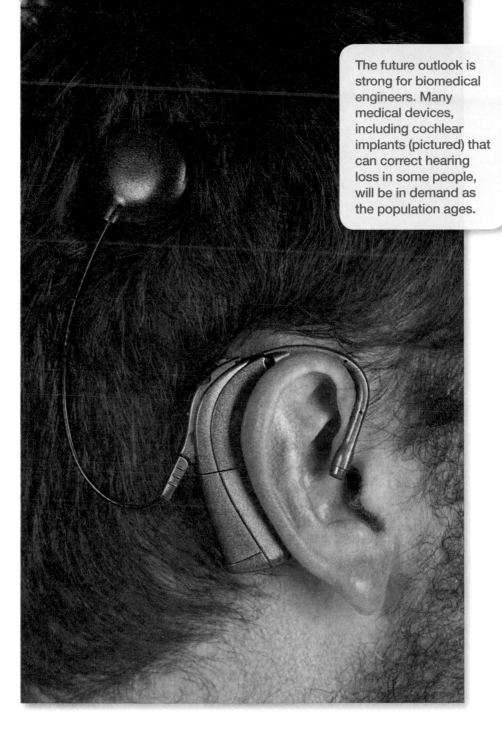

The future outlook is strong for biomedical engineers. Many medical devices, including cochlear implants (pictured) that can correct hearing loss in some people, will be in demand as the population ages.

dia, but also in social media, adding to the growing awareness of these cutting-edge treatments. "The future looks very bright [for biomedical engineering]," says Ravi Bellamkonda. "The impact of technology on medicine is dramatic, and incredible techniques are being developed. Yet there are still so many unmet needs that can be worked on and contributed to."[29]

Demand for innovative therapies is so great that in 2016, the FDA, the California Institute for Regenerative Medicine (CIRM), and the Sanford Stem Cell Clinical Center at UC San Diego Health all issued warnings to people who are turning to clinics that offer stem cell procedures that have not been proven safe and effective by the FDA. "Steer clear of them," says Lawrence Goldstein, director of the Sanford Stem Cell Clinical Center at UC San Diego Health. "They're probably taking advantage of you and it's probably unproven." Some clinics offer stem cell therapy for medical conditions such as Parkinson's and spinal cord injuries, as well as for cosmetic procedures such as breast augmentation. However, the only stem cell treatments currently approved by the FDA involve transplants from bone marrow or blood for patients with certain cancers and other disorders. "There are some really exciting developments showing great promise, but they are unproven at present,"[30] says Sidney Golub, director of the Sue and Bill Gross Stem Cell Research Center at the University of California, Irvine. More bioengineers are needed to develop safe and effective therapies.

Not only are demographics driving demand for bioengineered products, but also so is the pace of scientific discovery in the field of biomedicine. Scientists aided with high-powered computers working in the fields of genomics, proteomics, metabolomics, and systems biology are continually making breakthroughs about the root causes of disease. These discoveries are important unto themselves, but they must be translated into practical therapies if patients are to benefit from them. Bioengineers are essential to this process.

> "The future looks very bright [for biomedical engineering]. The impact of technology on medicine is dramatic, and incredible techniques are being developed. Yet there are still so many unmet needs that can be worked on and contributed to."[29]
>
> —Ravi Bellamkonda, chair of the biomedical engineering department at Georgia Tech and Emory University

Building an Artificial Human

In 2013 British roboticists Richard Walker and Matthew Godden assembled a human robot made of artificial organs, implants, limbs, and prosthetics developed by biomedical engineers. The robot was featured in the television program *How to Build a Bionic Man* and was displayed at London's Science Museum. The robot featured the following:

- An artificial heart that pumps a plastics-based blood replacement
- Artificial lungs that send oxygen into the bloodstream
- An artificial pancreas that secretes insulin to maintain healthy blood sugar levels
- An artificial kidney that uses living renal tubule cells from a healthy donor to filter the blood
- A pair of retinal implants for seeing
- A pair of cochlear implants for hearing
- A speech generator to talk
- Artificial arms, hands, legs, knees, ankles, and feet equipped with sensors that pick up the signals generated by muscular movements in the remaining limb to move the artificial limbs
- Brain implants that use computer chips to stimulate the brain and create memory

Some of these devices, such as the artificial heart and cochlear implants, are currently being used in human patients. Others, such as retinal implants, are being tested in human clinical trials. Still others, such as the artificial pancreas and artificial kidneys, exist but have not yet been approved for use in human beings. Artificial skin made of biomaterials and artificial windpipes grown from stem cells are also being tested for use in the future.

While most bioengineers stay in their field, some use their bioengineering degree to move into other fast-growing careers. For example, Sue-Mun Huang completed a bachelor's degree in biomedical engineering at the University of Auckland in New Zealand in 2012. In her final year of college, she worked as a student researcher for the Auckland Bioengineering Institute, investigating hypertensive heart disease. After graduation Huang worked as a clinical engineer in Auckland. In 2014 she moved to Toronto, Canada, and became a sales engineer at AdParlor, a company that offers a video and advertising platform for social media. "Having a professional engineering degree has really helped showcase my problem-solving abilities and adaptability," says Huang, "allowing an easy sidestep from scientific research into the software sector—and who knows what else next!"[31]

CHAPTER 7

Interview with a Biomedical Engineer

Sanket Goelis is an associate professor at Birla Institute of Technology and Science in Hyderabad, India. He has worked as a biomedical engineer for ten years. He answered questions about his career by e-mail.

Q: Why did you become a biomedical engineer?

A: To answer this question, I need to go back to 1999, when I did my master's degree science project at IIT Delhi, in optical science. I imagined pursuing my PhD in this field. However, I got an opportunity to do my PhD work in Alberta, Canada, where I started working on a project to develop devices to sort cells by suspending them in a very small stream of fluid and passing them by high-powered imaging equipment, a process known as flow cytometry. This was the beginning of my alignment of interest towards the biomedical domain and my evolution as a biomedical engineer/scientist.

My doctoral dissertation received attention from both industry and the scholarly community, including an e-mail from a principal investigator at Stanford University who invited me to do my postdoctoral research work there. I accepted the invitation and continued working in bioengineering. My work at Stanford led to future positions in the field. So, in summary, it was a chain reaction from the place I began my research career, and certainly the whole credit goes to my supervisors, co-workers, and students.

Q: Can you describe your typical workday?

A: I work in the academic environment. The academic life consists of three important facets—teaching, research, and administration—so I need to keep an appropriate and productive balance between these three domains. On the teaching front, I not only teach courses in a typical lecture setting, but I also teach tutorials and labs. It involves a lot of homework, in terms of preparing for lectures, laboratory problems, and evaluation. On the research front, one of the initial requirements is to create infrastructure and a team to implement the research projects. To this end, I'm involved in implementing funded projects but also in developing new funding proposals on a continuous basis. The research outcomes are presented in articles, patents, conference presentations, theses (PhD, PG, and UG), and various reports. The academic administration duties include leading various policy-making initiatives and then implementing them. In addition, I contribute towards multiple scientific activities, such as reviewing and examining academic activities from other organizations, delivering popular and scientific talks, and participating in various academic committees. Therefore, a typical workday includes a variety of aforementioned facets, which of course differ on a given workday.

Q: What do you like most about your job?

A: The thing I like most about my job is the amount of flexibility given to balance your professional and personal life. Working in academia, I get to pursue the research I am most interested in. I work in developing micro-devices and nanomaterials for targeted DNA sequencing; conversion of microorganisms to energy; and biomedical diagnostics, such as glucose sensing for diabetes diagnostics, TB diagnostics, and cancer diagnostics.

Q: What do you like least about your job?

A: Frankly, I don't dislike anything in particular. The work is so fulfilling, satisfying, and productive that the joy I have at the end of the day gives me an extra smile in the evening and a comfortable night's sleep to make myself ready for the following day. Of course, there are challenges to performing such multidimensional work. One such challenge is how to get things moving among various stakeholders. Developing a good professional rapport with all the stakeholders is essential.

Q: What personal qualities do you find most valuable for this type of work?

A: I believe my jovial and simple personality works as a catalyst to deal with various facets of my job in an efficient manner. In fact, I believe that such qualities are a must for any person working in any work of life. Furthermore, I have a "can-do" spirit; I try to get the work done without giving up. I also feel that having a simple, friendly human nature certainly adds flavor to one's daily life, and it also helps when searching for reasonable and applicable answers to various challenges.

Q: What advice do you have for students who might be interested in this career?

A: My advice is to dream. We must dream, and we must have vision for ourselves. Based on such dreams and visions, we must then plan to succeed. Of course, at times, our plan might not be optimally productive, but we can always think about an alternate approach. Since biomedical engineering is a multidisciplinary domain, it is imperative to keep up with the most recent happenings and outputs in the field and related scientific domains. Of course practical applications play an important role in what I do, but a student should have a good understanding of the biological and engineering fundamentals. Keeping ourselves busy is extremely important, as only busy people can do more and better things for the society at large.

SOURCE NOTES

Introduction: Developing Technology to Treat Disease

1. Quoted in American Institute for Medical and Biological Engineering, "Joyce Wong Interview," Meet Inspiring Bioengineers. http://navigate.aimbe.org.
2. World Health Organization, "Controlling the Global Obesity Epidemic." www.who.int.
3. Quoted in Anne Trafton, "Fat-Fighting Nanoparticles: New Drug-Delivery Approach Holds Potential for Treating Obesity," MIT News, May 2, 2016. http://news.mit.edu.
4. Quoted in American Institute for Medical and Biological Engineering, "Joyce Wong Interview."

Chapter 1: What Does a Biomedical Engineer Do?

5. Quoted in Bioengineering University of California, Berkeley, "Faculty Working in Bioinstrumentation: Michael Yartsev." http://bioeng.berkeley.edu.
6. Quoted in American Institute for Medical and Biological Engineering, "Robert Langer Interview," Meet Inspiring Bioengineers. http://navigate.aimbe.org.
7. Quoted in American Institute for Medical and Biological Engineering, "Gilda Barabino Interview," Meet Inspiring Bioengineers. http://navigate.aimbe.org.
8. Quoted in American Institute for Medical and Biological Engineering, "Tom Chau Interview," Meet Inspiring Bioengineers. http://navigate.aimbe.org.
9. Quoted in Christopher J. Gearon, "Explore Biomedical Engineering, Other Hot Jobs for Future Engineers," *U.S. News & World Report*, March 25, 2016. www.usnews.com.
10. Quoted in Science Buddies, "Science Careers: Interview with Katie Hilpisch." www.sciencebuddies.org.

Chapter 2: How Do You Become a Biomedical Engineer?

11. Quoted in American Institute for Medical and Biological Engineering, "Tom Chau Interview."

12. Quoted in American Institute for Medical and Biological Engineering, "Gilda Barabino Interview."

Chapter 3: What Skills and Personal Qualities Are Important to a Biomedical Engineer?

13. Quoted in American Institute for Medical and Biological Engineering, "Gilda Barabino Interview."
14. Quoted in American Institute for Medical and Biological Engineering, "Fernando Cordova Interview," Meet Inspiring Bioengineers. http://navigate.aimbe.org.
15. Quoted in American Institute for Medical and Biological Engineering, "Ravi Bellamkonda Interview," Meet Inspiring Bioengineers. http://navigate.aimbe.org.
16. Quoted in American Institute for Medical and Biological Engineering, "Robert Langer Interview."
17. Quoted in American Institute for Medical and Biological Engineering, "Gilda Barabino Interview."
18. Quoted in American Institute for Medical and Biological Engineering, "Gilda Barabino Interview."
19. Quoted in American Institute for Medical and Biological Engineering, "Ravi Bellamkonda Interview."
20. Quoted in American Institute for Medical and Biological Engineering, "Ravi Bellamkonda Interview."
21. Quoted in TryEngineering, "Lori Laird: Biomedical Engineer." www.tryengineering.org.
22. Quoted in National Academy of Engineering, "Interviews: Kay C. Dee," EngineerGirl, January 11, 2008. www.engineergirl.org.

Chapter 4: What Is It Like to Work as a Biomedical Engineer?

23. Quoted in American Institute for Medical and Biological Engineering, "Robert Langer Interview."
24. Quoted in American Institute for Medical and Biological Engineering, "Robert Langer Interview."
25. Quoted in Science Buddies, "Science Careers: Interview with Katie Hilpisch."
26. Quoted in TryEngineering, "Lori Laird: Biomedical Engineer."

Chapter 5: Advancement and Other Job Opportunities

27. Quoted in American Institute for Medical and Biological Engineering, "Gilda Barabino Interview."
28. Quoted in National Academy of Engineering, "Interviews: Kay C. Dee."

Chapter 6: What Does the Future Hold for Biomedical Engineers?

29. Quoted in American Institute for Medical and Biological Engineering, "Ravi Bellamkonda Interview."
30. Quoted in Emily Bazar, "Beware of Unapproved Stem Cell Treatments," *California Healthline*, September 30, 2016. www.californiahealthline.org.
31. Quoted in "Careers in Professional Engineering," Youth Futures Hawkes Bay, July 2016. http://youthfutures.co.nz/wp-content/uploads/2014/12/Profiles-of-Professional-Engineers-July-2016.pdf.

FIND OUT MORE

American Institute for Medical and Biological Engineering (AIMBE)

1400 I St. NW, Suite 235
Washington, DC 20005
website: http://navigate.aimbe.org

The AIMBE is a nonprofit organization that advocates for medical and biological engineers. Its "Navigate the Circuit" website is designed to help students of all levels with video interviews with prominent biomedical engineers, overviews of various specializations and career pathways, and a school search tool for undergraduate and graduate biomedical engineering students that can be narrowed by state and by degree type—biomedical or biological.

Biomedical Engineering Society (BMES)

8201 Corporate Dr., Suite 1125
Landover, MD 20785
website: www.bmes.org

The BMES is the world's leading society of professionals devoted to developing and using engineering and technology to advance human health. It communicates recent advances, discoveries, and inventions through journals and conferences and promotes education and professional development through workshops and e-learning.

EngineerGirl

National Academy of Engineering
500 Fifth St. NW, Room 1047
Washington, DC 20001
website: www.engineergirl.org

Created by the National Academy of Engineering, the Engineer-Girl website is designed to bring national attention to the exciting opportunities that engineering represents for girls and women.

It features short profiles of 294 female engineers; dozens of in-depth interviews; and areas devoted to "Ask an Engineer," "A Day in the Life," and "Historical Engineers."

National Institute of Biomedical Imaging and Bioengineering (NIBIB)
9000 Rockville Pike
Bethesda, MD 20892
website: www.nibib.nih.gov

Part of the National Institutes of Health, the NIBIB seeks to improve health through research and development of new biomedical imaging and bioengineering techniques and devices to fundamentally improve the detection, treatment, and prevention of disease. The website includes resource links for students, parents, and teachers; news and videos; and training information.

Science Buddies
Sobrato Center for Nonprofits
560 Valley Way
Milpitas, CA 95035
website: www.sciencebuddies.org

Created to help students build their literacy in science and technology, the Science Buddies website contains more than fifteen thousand pages of scientist-developed subject matter (including experiments based on the latest academic research) and an online community of science professionals who volunteer to advise students. They also provide resources to support parents and teachers as they guide students doing hands-on science projects.

PICTURE CREDITS

ABOUT THE AUTHOR

Bradley Steffens is an award-winning poet, playwright, novelist, and author of more than thirty nonfiction books for children and young adults. He is a two-time recipient of the San Diego Book Award for Best Young Adult and Children's Nonfiction: His *Giants* won the 2005 award, and his *J.K. Rowling* claimed the 2007 prize. Steffens also received the Theodor S. Geisel Award for best book by a San Diego County author in 2007.